15

A Trip To The Seaside
A Story Book With Makaton

Foreword

The following guidance is intended to help you enjoy reading with your child and benefit from using Makaton.

If your child is new to reading you may find it helpful to begin with our 'My First Makaton' range of picture books. These simple books are designed to help your child become familiar with reading materials including how a book is held, and that pages are turned in sequence starting from the front cover towards the back.

The text throughout the story is accompanied by Makaton. Using Makaton when reading with your child helps them follow and understand the story.

With Makaton, speech is always used when signing. Therefore signs should be made while reading aloud to your child.

Additional signs are included towards the back of this book to help you discuss and explore the illustrations with your child.

Tips & Guidance

When reading this book please remember the following key points;

- Reading should be a fun and pleasurable experience. Don't worry if your child does not want to read. Let them listen and allow your enthusiasm for the story attract their interest.

- Choose a time of day for reading and include this in your normal routine. For example after lunchtime or at bedtime. Most children benefit from a routine and look forward to story time.

- Encourage your child to read and/or sign along with you based on their recall. It is very natural for children to do this.

- Allow your child to choose what they would like to read. Don't worry if they keep choosing the same book. Reading the same story over and over again helps them learn and should be encouraged. It is important to maintain your interest in the story as this will in turn hold your child's attention.

- Try to learn the signs before you start to read with your child.

- Intonation and body language are an essential part of using Makaton. Use eye contact and facial expressions as you are signing to provide essential meaning and context.

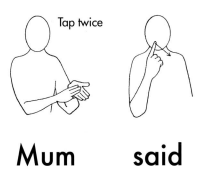

Mum   **said**

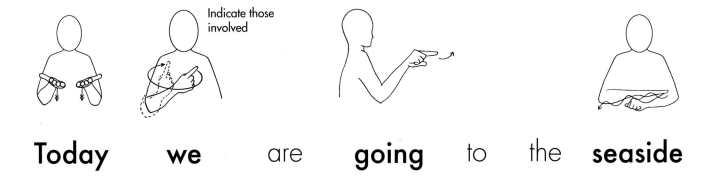

Today   **we**   are   **going**   to   the   **seaside**

4

5

Tap twice

Direct sign towards person

Mum   asked

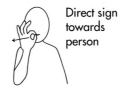

Where   is   your   swimming costume?

The   **girl**   **said**

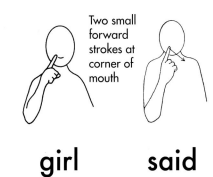

Two small forward strokes at corner of mouth

My   **swimming costume**   is   on   the   **bed**

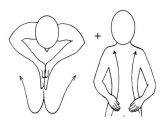

Eyes open

9

Finger moves
slowly from
wrist to elbow

The **cars** are **going** **slowly**

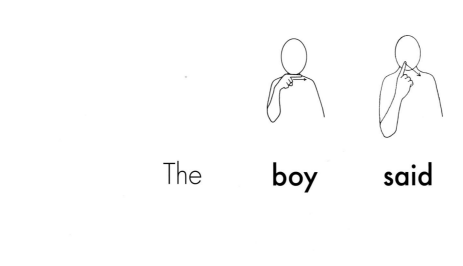

The **boy** **said**

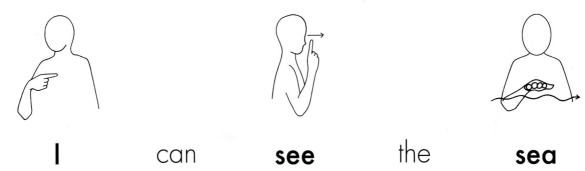

I can **see** the **sea**

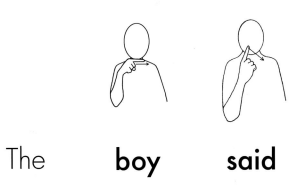

The **boy** said

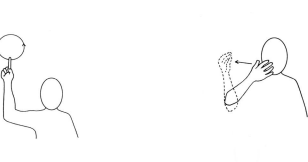

The **sun** is **hot**

15

The **boy** said

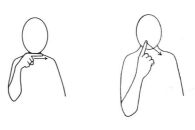

Draw formation towards body

Help me **build** a **sandcastle**

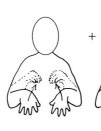

+

Mime sifting sand through fingers

17

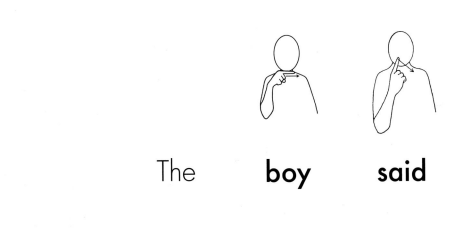

The **boy** **said**

Mime licking ice cream

I **would like** an **ice cream** please

The **girl** **said**

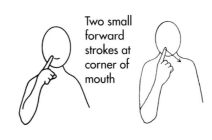

Two small forward strokes at corner of mouth

I am **riding** a **donkey**

Progress movement forwards

Flat hands flap down and up at wrists

21

Tap Twice

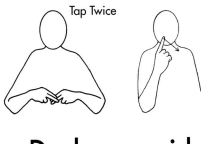

Dad   said

Tap twice

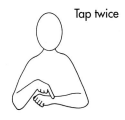

Small arced movement - direction can be varied to suit context

It's   **time**   to   **go**   **home**

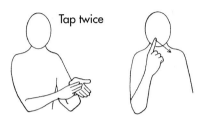

Tap twice

Mum   **said**

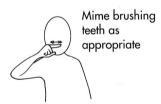

Mime brushing teeth as appropriate

Brush your teeth

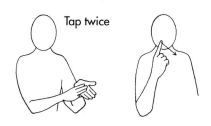

Mum **said**

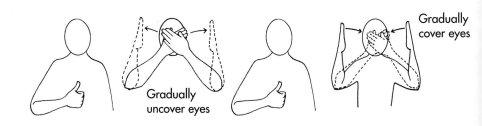

It's   been   a   **lovely**   **day**   **good**   **night**

Other Useful Signs

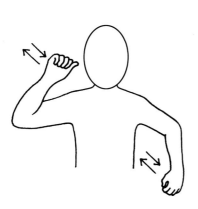

Towel

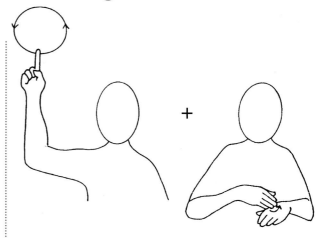

Sun cream

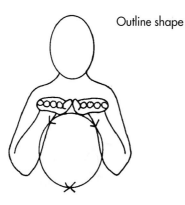

Outline shape

Ball

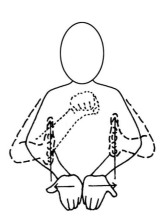

Bucket